1 MONTH OF
FREE
READING
at
www.ForgottenBooks.com

By purchasing this book you are eligible for one month membership to ForgottenBooks.com, giving you unlimited access to our entire collection of over 1,000,000 titles via our web site and mobile apps.

To claim your free month visit:
www.forgottenbooks.com/free899998

ISBN 978-0-265-85628-4
PIBN 10899998

A STUDY OF THE INFLUENCE OF TEMPERATURE ON WHEAT
TEMPERING

by

ROYCE OWEN PENCE

B. S., Kansas State Agricultural College, 1924

————

A THESIS

submitted in partial fulfillment of the

requirements for the degree of

MASTER OF SCIENCE

KANSAS STATE AGRICULTURAL COLLEGE

1930

TABLE OF CONTENTS

INTRODUCTION

Tempering is the process of conditioning wheat by the adding or removing of water, for the purpose of toughening the germ and bran; also making the endosperm or floury portion of the berry more friable. Another way to define tempering would be the changing of wheat into such a physical condition that the separation of the bran from the endosperm is facilitated, and whereby so far as is possible the baking quality of the resulting flour shall be improved.

Since the two principal objects in tempering are to bring the wheat into a suitable condition for mechanical treatment in the mill, and to improve the baking qualities of the flour, the results of good milling, as influenced by tempering, may be seen and judged more easily than those associated with the flour quality. It is also evident if the first object of tempering is not achieved, the baking quality of the flour will suffer indirectly; for the presence of bran powder in the flour, as an example, lowers the general quality of the flour. The color of the flour being poor, and due to the harmful enzymes introduced along with the bran, the baking value of the flour is seriously depreciated. Hence the miller should remember that in tempering there are two objects, and in order to achieve excellence in the one he should see that the other does not suffer.

The problem of tempering developed when Turkey wheat was first grown on the western plains, where the dry weather during the ripening period produced a hard vitreous kernel. This made it impossible to separate the floury portion from the bran and germ, so as to produce as white a flour as was produced from soft wheat.

In the United States we think of tempering as adding water to the wheat, while in some of the foreign countries it is necessary to reduce the moisture content of the grain before milling. It is generally accepted among millers that wheat with approximately 15 per cent of moisture is the best for grinding. Slight variations must be made due to the physical texture of the grain and flinctuation in relative humidity during milling.

Automatic devices have been invented to add the water to the wheat before putting it in tempering bins; where it stands from six to seventy-two hours. For mills of 1000 to 6000 barrels daily capacity the longer time necessitates enormous bin space to hold the wheat during tempering. The loss may also be considerable if the mill breaks down so the wheat cannot be milled for several days, since heating may occur due to excess moisture.

In many mills wheat heaters are used during the cold weather to heat the wheat before tempering, and some use

these heaters the year round. Since the chemical con-
stituency and the physical properties of the bran, germ,
and endosperm are so different, wheat may be conditioned to
a certain extent by the use of heat alone. As the temperature of the wheat is increased the physical texture of the
wheat is changed, the endosperm becomes softer, while the
germ and bran become less friable. These changes help to
accomplish the requirements of tempering.

Temperature also influences the rate of movement of
the water molecules. The higher temperature not only
speeds the action of these molecules, but increases the
distance between them, which will increase the rate at
which water will penetrate the grain.

In 19⬛ a device called a temperator was pattented by
the General Mill Equipment Company, in which the wheat is
heated in the process of tempering. Experiments have been
conducted with the apparatus, and it is claimed that wheat
can be tempered with it in thirty minutes. If it is
possible to temper wheat in that length of time, it will
mean a great economic saving both in time and building
space. It will also eliminate the uncertainties in tempering wheat to suit the weather conditions of to-day, and
then finding them changed at the actual time of milling.

In a survey of tempering practice in the different
mills, a letter was mailed from the college to 144 mills.
Eighty-eight of these mills answered this letter, some
omitting the answers to part of the questions. Seventy-
six of these mills ground hard wheat and 34 were using
heat in connection with tempering, 7 of the 34 used heat
the entire year while 37 used heat only during cold weather,
which shows that using heat is considered by some practical,
although they may not be using it to the best economical
advantage.

The experiments reported in this thesis are divided
into three groups: water penetration, work on the experimental mill, and work on the large mill. The former mill
is non-automatic, and the sample milled is five pounds
or less. The large mill is the long system mill of 60
barrels capacity.

ACKNOWLEDGMENTS

Acknowledgment is hereby given to my major instructors
Dr. C.O. Swanson and Dr. E.B. Working, for their many
suggestions and criticisms, often going out of their way
in order to help solve some problem dealing with my work.

Parts of the experiment were impossible to conduct alone, so acknowledgment is hereby given to Mr. R.E. McCormick and Mr. C.W. Oakes for their assistance when called upon to assist in the experiments.

Acknowledgment is given to the Milling Department for the use of the data in connection with the water penetration experiment. Part of this data had been collected under the direction of Dr. C.O. Swanson. This was given before the annual millers' meeting at Manhattan, 1930 and published in the May issue 1930 of the American Miller. Acknowledgment is also given to the Milling Department for the unlimited use of all equipment in the different laboratories of the department.

REVIEW OF LITERATURE

In reviewing current literature in milling magazines, we find that most statements are based upon the conclusions which the authors have made from rather casual observations. As a rule, no data is offered to substantiate the statements made. The knowledge of the best conditions for tempering is still fragmentary, as far as scientifically conducted investigations are concerned.

Amos (1920) states that conditioning of wheat is the process of lining up various wheats in a mixture to the same degree of hardness, toughness and mellowness, so that

each individual grain shall stand the same breaking down
on the rolls, with approximately the same results; in
large bran flakes, small percentage of break flour, and
plenty of good bright semolina and middlings. There shall
be no bran powder (due to brittle skins and too small
percentage of water) and no pasty juicy bran, stained
flour and lost flour in the offals (due to too great a
percentage of water.)

Fagus (1920) states that in tempering wheat at 5°, 20°,
and 40°C., for the periods of 24, 48, and 72 hours.
At the temperature of 5°C. the length of tempering period
appeared to have very little influence on either the
physical characteristics or the chemical composition of the
flour.

When the wheat was tempered at 20°C., a small but
definite chemical change took place. The hydrogen-ion
concentration was increased, as shown by the lower P_H
figure. The total acidity, the water soluble phosphorus
and the titrable nitrogen were also higher. Both the yield
and the milling qualities were better than when the wheat
was tempered at 5°C. The time of tempering appeared to be
a factor in the chemical changes, but had very little if
any relation to the physical characteristics.

The chemical changes were still more pronounced when
the wheat was tempered at 40°C. The physical changes,

however, appeared to be detrimental to the milling qualities of the grain.

Simon (1923) states that the four direct results of good conditioning are:

1. To toughen the bran and to prevent bran powder being formed.
2. To secure the easiest separation of the bran from the endosperm.
3. To render easy the subsequent breaking down of the endosperm.
4. To get accurate and easy sifting on the dressing machines.

He also states that owing to the risk of damage, the bulk of the wheat ought not to be heated to a temperature higher than 40°C. as otherwise some individual grains might reach 60°C. at which temperature rapid and far-reaching changes may occur which may be very harmful.

In order to get quick and effective conditioning or tempering of the wheat so that it grinds nicely on the rolls the wheat ought to be heated to not less than 43°C.

Dunham (1925) states that with the knowledge of how the endosperm of the wheat berry is built up, the function of the hollow hairs and the structural resistance of the skins to prevent the entrance of moisture to the endosperm except through the hollow hairs— for the entrance by the

placenta is closed and sealed by the two hairy valves
(the valve however can be displaced by friction in the
cleaning department of the mill) that water can enter only
through the hair of the grain. It is at once apparent how
washing, drying, and chilling the grain are simply carry-
ing out a natural law by going one step forward in develop-
ing the wheat in the mill as well as making the grain more
uniform and improving the resultant flour.

Lewellen (1927) states that their observations lead
them to state that the ideal temperature of a finished
flour at the agitators is between 21° and $27^\circ C$. That below
$21^\circ C$ the miller cannot get the proper dress, clean up, or
yield, and that too much of the feed is included in the
flour. That above $27^\circ C$. the flour is too hot in that mold
growth may start, chemical and enzymatic changes will be
started which will result in rancidity, increased acidity
and deterioration of gluten.

Kent-Jones (1927) experimented with wheat dampened to
a moisture content of 17-18 per cent placing it in enclosed
rectangular tin slots about one inch in width, and these
were put in a water bath which was kept at the desired
temperature for a definite time. In this way dampened
Manitoba wheat was heated at $32^\circ C$. for periods of 30 minutes to 24 hours. No substantial difference was found

between the wheats heated for 30 minutes to 24 hours.

The experiment was repeated at 43°C. and again it was found that no chemical change apparently occurred under the conditions of the experiment at that temperature for as long as 24 hours. In no case were the baking qualities affected.

In heating the dampened wheat at 57°C. it was found that no chemical or physical changes were apparent. It must be remembered that the whole of the wheat would not be at that temperature all the time. The outside portions soon acquired a temperature 1 or 2° below that of the bath, but the center portions took some time to reach the maximum temperature.

In continuing the heating at 57°C. for six hours it was found that slight chemical changes took place, but very little change could be observed in the baking test. When the heating was continued for 24 hours, however, a definite change occurred which was indicated by the baking test, the strength of the flour being improved. In a few hours the flour developed a disagreeable sour odor.

Samples then were heated to 71°C. for 1½ to 2 hours and then cooled before adding the tempering water. The wheat appeared to be unchanged, but later when it was conditioned and ground into flour, the flour was found to have increased strength.

As the protein of most wheats appears to be in an insufficient degree of coagulation or aggregation, it can be greatly improved by a subsequent heat coagulation, before undergoing the process of milling.

Swanson (1928) states that carefully controlled use of heat on fully matured, but new wheat, will bring about an improvement in the baking qualities. However, if the degree of temperature is too high, or if the period of heating is too long, marked damage may result.

When heating takes place under uncontrolled conditions such as happens when wheat is cut immature, serious damage may result. The same will apply to wheat cut too wet but fully mature. Controlled heating will improve immature wheat when the degree of temperature is not too high or the period of heating too long.

McCormick (1930) states that he found very little difference if any in the influence of the length of tempering at ordinary temperatures of around 25 to 30°C. upon the process of milling or upon the resultant flour as determined by the baking methods.

RATE OF WATER PENETRATION IN WHEAT DURING TEMPERING

In a survey which was conducted by the Milling
Department it was found that in commercial practice the ex-
tremes in time of tempering are from 3 hours to 72 hours.
If the water gets to the center of the wheat kernel and is
uniformly distributed in a short length of time, why the
many hours of tempering? The object of this investigation
was to learn how soon the tempering water becomes evenly
distributed throughout the endosperm.

In analysing the water penetration in wheat during
tempering, it may be well to define the words adsorb and
absorb, before going too far in this discussion. The
definition may help to avoid confusion of the two terms
since they are spelled and sound so similar. These definitions are taken from the New Century dictionary: Adsorb
means to gather on the surface of the molecules in a con-
densed layer, while absorb means to take up by chemical or
molecular action. According to these definitions, absorption takes place when the water penetrates the wheat kernel,
and may take place under the following conditions: When
the wheat is immersed or dipped in water, and when water is
added as in tempering, that is, when a small amount of
water is added to the wheat and thoroughly mixed. Water is
also absorbed when wheat is exposed to air of a high humidity.

Absorption when Wheat is Immersed in Water

To determine the rate of absorption when wheat is totally submerged in water for varying lengths of time and in water of different temperatures, a definite amount of wheat was immersed in the water at a controlled temperature for a given length of time. Then it was placed in specially made cups with screens on the bottoms. These cups were then placed in a centrifuge and the surface water thrown off by centrifugal force. The centrifuge used was an ordinary Babcock cream tester. It was turned at a given rate and for the same length of time in every determination.

In order to eliminate error from evaporation in these experiments, two cups were centrifuged at a time, then weighed before starting to centrifuge the next two. A uniform lot of hard wheat was used. By this method it is believed that very comparative data was obtained. In a preliminary trial, four samples were treated alike in order to determine if comparable results could be obtained. The figures in Table I give the variation which occurred in this series of tests, and shows the limits of accuracy for the figures obtained in the trials which are reported in this thesis.

Table I Variations in the amounts of water absorbed under similar conditions.

Time of soaking	Grams of water absorbed by 100 gm. of wheat at indoor temperature.				Maximum difference	Average	Maximum deviation from average.	Probable error	Ratio D/P.E.
10 minutes	6.88	6.7	6.84	6.78	.18	6.80	.066	.067	.08
30 minutes	10.44	10.26	10.28	10.46	.22	10.35	.115	.067	.17
40 minutes	12.54	11.62	11.96	11.88	.72	12.07	.465	.067	.70
18 hours	46.56	46.14	46.52	46.40	.42	46.40	.285	.067	.39

The greatest difference between the maximum and mini-
mum in these single trials was .72 gm., and the least .15 gm.
or the variation was less than one gram of the amount of
water absorbed by the wheat. However, one must determine
if these errors are significant, or if more trials are
necessary in order to obtain sufficient accuracy. In order
to make this clear it will be necessary to find the deviation from the average, and also its ratio to the probable
error. The largest deviation from the average of each four
trials was .465 gm., and for the ten minutes it was .065
gm., which is very small. The ratio of deviation to probable
error should be less than three if an experiment does not
need more trials for reliable information. To determine the
probable error, it is first necessary to calculate the
standard deviation of the point binomial using the formula
$S = \sqrt{npq}$, where S is the standard deviation of the point
binomial, n is the number of trials and p is the probability
of accuracy, while q is the probability of inaccuracy.

The probability of a complete set of compound events
may be illustrated by bossing up a coin. The probability
that heads will turn up during a number of trials will be
a fifty-fifty chance -- or p and q each will be equal to .5.
The same is true with experimental work. One has a fifty-
fifty chance of accuracy on each test.

Now since the probable error is equal to .6745 times
the standard deviation of the point binomial, the probable
error is equal to .6745 $\sqrt{.5 \times .5n}$ or .3375 $\sqrt{n}$. Substituting
1/3 for .33725 , we have the probable error equal to $1/3\sqrt{n}$.
The probable error then equals $1/3\sqrt{4}$ or .667 , while the
largest deviation from the average is the difference from
the average and the trial farthest away from the average.
The ratio of deviation to probable error is found by dividing the deviation by its probable error. This ratio of the
deviation from the mean to its probable error is less than
one in all cases, as shown in the last column of Table I.
In fact, the largest ratio is .7 for the 40 minutes of
soaking the grain, which indicates very good experimental
results. Consequently, the data obtained under these
experimental conditions may be considered reliable.

This data shows that in ten minutes at room temperatures, the wheat had taken up 6.8 per cent of its original
weight in water. In thirty minutes it had gained 10.33 per
cent of its original weight. This is not three times the
amount absorbed in ten minutes, but is an average of .17 of
one per cent per minute after the first ten minutes. We
notice that in the next ten minutes it gains in a similar
ratio, but as the time increased the amount of water absorbed
decreased in proportion. In other words, wheat immersed in

water absorbs it rapidly at first, thereafter as the length of time increases the amount of water absorbed gradually decreases, that is, as the wheat becomes filled with water, the rate of absorption diminishes. At the end of fifteen hours it had gained 46.46 per cent of its original weight, or nearly all the water possible for it to hold.

Tests were also made to ascertain the influence that temperature has upon the rate of water penetration. Experiments were conducted, heating and cooling wheat and water to given temperatures before immersing the wheat in the water. The following temperatures were used: 6^{0}, 27^{0}, 40^{0}, 60^{0} and $80^{0}C$. Time of immersion was varied at the lower temperatures from just dipping the wheat into the water to soaking it for 48 hours. For the higher temperatures it was not soaked over such long periods, but in all cases the wheat was heated or cooled to temperature of the water before submerging. The length of time for immersion recorded was from the time the wheat was submerged until it was taken from the water bath. The cups holding the wheat were then immediately placed in the centrifuge and whirled. The figures in Table II are the averages from four determinations.

The instant dipping trial was done to determine the amount of water that would cling to the grain. Just how much of this entered the interior of the grain is impossible to say, but the samples showed over four per cent gain in

Table II Effect of temperature in water penetration

Duration of immersion in water.	Grams of water absorbed per 100 mm. of wheat. Temperatures.								
	6°C.	27°C.	36°C.	40°C.	60°C.	80°C. : Mean	:Largest deviation	:D./P.E.
Instant dipping:	4.1	4.5	5.4	4.1	4.1	4.1 : 4.04	.64	.86
10 seconds	4.1	5.1	4.6	4.4	4.7 : 4.48	.52	.70
20 seconds	4.6	5.6	5.0	4.5	5.5 : 5.0	.6	.81
40 seconds	5.4	6.5	5.1	4.9	5.5 : 5.3	1.0	1.34
1 minute	5.5	7.3	7.4	5.7	5.5 : 6.44	1.04	1.40
8 minutes	5.6	7.7	8.4	7.8	8.0 : 7.52	1.58	2.44
5 minutes	5.7	8.9	10.0	10.0	14.1 : 9.84	4.56	6.12
10 minutes	6.8	9.9	11.7	14.7	22.1			
20 minutes	6.9	12.0	15.7	20.5	33.7			
40 minutes	9.1	14.3	19.9	29.5	46.7			
90 minutes	10.6	18.6	29.6	45.5				
8 hours	12.5	21.1	32.2	49.7				
3 hours	14.5	24.4	36.6					
4 hours	15.4	29.6	40.7					
6 hours	20.1	33.2	45.3					
8 hours	23.5	39.4	49.1					
16 hours	24.7	45.5						
24 hours	27.8	50.4						
48 hours	35.8							

weight. The 10 seconds immersion shows only a slight increase in gain of water over the instant dipping, although
the average for the various temperatures is one-half per
cent greater. No material increase is noted at the higher
temperatures for the short periods of time, which indicates
that temperature effect is very small on the amount of
water absorbed when the time is short. If we apply the ratio
of the deviation from the mean to the probable error in the
analysis and comparison of this data we find that the
temperature does not enter into the results until the grain
has soaked more than 2 minutes. Our comparison of the
deviation from the mean to the probable error is only .86
for instant dipping, but at 2 minutes soaking its ratio is
2.66; at 5 minutes soaking it is 6.12. This shows that after
2 minutes soaking there is a marked difference in the
effect of temperature upon the rate of absorption of water
by the grain. Since the ratio will increase with the time
of soaking it was not calculated for the rest of the data.

Table II also shows that the wheat absorbed 5.6 gm. of
water in 2 minutes at 6°C., while at 80°C. 9 gm. was
absorbed, or 3.4 gm. more, due to the higher temperature.
The wheat at 80°C. absorbed its maximum amount of water in
40 minutes; at 60°C. it took 2 hours; at 40°C 8 hours;
while at 27°C. (a little above average room temperature) it
took 24 hours, and at 6°). the maximum was not reached in

48 hours. This shows that heat plays an important part in the rate at which water will penetrate the wheat, at least when the amount of water is large. The surface tension of the water is reduced by warming and thus it will penetrate much more rapidly. For example, place a few drops of cold water on a board, then put an equal amount of warm or hot water on the same board, and note how much more readily the warm or hot water seeks into the board. The same is true of wheat, as shown in this experiment.

Some people believe that wheat is surrounded by a non-permeable membrane, but if it were, as is the case of white clover seed, it would not absorb water. Because white clover seed does not germinate readily, it was thought by some people that the seed was poor, but it was found that the slow germination was due to the non-permeable membrane which covers the grain. After scarifying the seed nearly all of it would germinate. Wheat does not need to be scarified to enable moisture to come into contact with the endosperm, as water can be absorbed very readily through the bran coat, germination taking place in twenty-four to forty-eight hours time if there is sufficient moisture and the temperature is suitable.

Coating Wheat with Shellac to Determine where the Water
Enters the Berry

An experiment was conducted to find out if water
enters the wheat kernel more easily at one place than
another. Head samples of Kanred wheat were obtained. Each
grain was picked from the head separately so that the bran
coat, or any non-permeable membrane, that might surround the
kernels would not be scratched. This wheat was divided
into four lots, one used as a check sample; one shellacked
on the germ; one on the brush end, and one on the back of
the grain. In each case approximately equal parts of the
wheat surface was covered. After the shellac had dried,
each sample was weighed and then placed between wet layers
of muslin which was first soaked in water, then wrung to
remove excess moisture. This wheat was removed for weighing at the following intervals: 1, 2, 4, 6, and 24 hours.
As soon as taken from the wet muslin the kernels were
placed between blotters to remove surface water, then they
were weighed, and placed again between the wet cloth.
Water was added at intervals to the cloths in order to
keep the moisture uniform during the experiment. Table III
shows the per cent gain in these samples for the various
periods of time.

Table III Water penetration through different parts of
bran coat showing the per cent gain.

Sample	Hours				
	1	2	4	6	24
Check	5.8	8.5	13.6	18.4	40.0
Shellac on brush	6.3	9.3	14.1	20.8	37.8
Shellac on back	4.3	6.9	10.5	14.1	32.0
Shellac on germ	4.1	6.2	9.3	12.6	29.7

At one hour of soaking the wheat treated with shellac
on the brush absorbed 6.3 per cent moisture, while the
check sample absorbed only 5.8 per cent. The grain treated
with shellac on the germ absorbed 4.1 per cent, and that
treated on the back gained 4.3 per cent. The fact that the
absorption in the kernels whose brush ends were covered
with shellac was as great as the check sample which was
without shellac on any part, shows that very little if any
absorption took place through the brush end. This state-
ment will not hold for kernels which have been threshed or
scoured. The kernels shellacked on germ or back absorbed
less water than those shellacked on brush end. In fact very
little difference is noticed in the samples shellacked on
germ or on the back. The theory advanced by some

people that water enters only through the germ does not
hold in the face of these figures, and it must be admitted
that water enters the grain throughout the whole bran coat.
The non absorption through the brush end in hand plucked
kernels is probably due to the film of air held by the
fine wheat hairs, or to the increased resistance due to
the excess friction.

Rate of Water Absorption in Tempering Wheat.

Water is added to wheat in tempering for two reasons:
to make the bran coat tougher, and to mellow the endosperm.
These will be considered in this experiment. The experiments already given show that the water enters the wheat
kernel rather rapidly, and the rate is increased by higher
temperatures. In tempering, the water is applied in a man-
ner altogether different from that of immersing the wheat
in water as used in the above experiments. Although the
fundamental principles in regard to absorption are similar,
whether it enters as rapidly in the process of tempering
is a question to be answered. Also we need to determine
if all that is necessary in tempering is merely distri-
buting the water through the berry. While the amount of
water is comparatively small, yet the absorption may be
just as complete. Whether more of this water is absorbed
by the bran than by the endosperm must also be determined,

also how much of this water is lost during the tempering process.

Presumably a certain amount of absorption of a chemical nature takes place during the process of tempering. This may help change the physical texture of the endosperm. This part of the problem is not considered in this paper. Such absorption would have an effect on the colloidal behavior of the flour and on the baking qualities.

The rate of absorption in tempering for various periods may be determined by adding a definite amount of water to a weighed quantity of wheat of known moisture content, and determining the moisture in the cracked wheat, bran, and various sized middlings.

For this experiment a uniform lot of Turkey wheat of a known moisture content was used. It was first cleaned on a small experimental separator, then scoured on a small Eureka experimental scourer. For each test 800 gm. of wheat was placed in each of three half gallon Mason jars. Enough water was added to bring the moisture content up to 16.75 per cent as determined by drying at 130°C. for one hour and 15 minutes, which gives approximately 1.25 per cent more moisture than by the Brown Duvel method. Therefore by common methods the wheat had 15.5 per cent moisture which is considered optimum. The periods of tempering were 1, 2, 4, 8, 16, and 24 hours, and the time

of tempering was so regulated that the wheat could be
ground at the expiration of the period set for each sample.
This experiment was conducted during the winter months
when a relatively low temperature could be maintained with
a humidity of about 60 per cent. The evaporation is not
as great under these conditions as it is at higher temperatures, even with higher humidities.

Five hundred grams of the tempered wheat was used for
milling, and the rest for moisture determination on each
sample of wheat milled. The wheat was first passed through
the break rolls set at .028 inches apart, which corresponds
to our first break, and then immediately passed through the
rolls at .006 inches apart, corresponding to our third
break grinding. Then the sample was sifted immediately,
taking less than 5 minutes from the time grinding was
started until sifting was completed. This insured only
a small loss in weight due to evaporation of moisture.
There was also a possibility of a small mechanical loss.
The following stack of sieves were used during sifting:
24 wire, 30 G.G. and 70 G.G. The stocks as well as the
wheat were weighed on a balance sensitive to 0.1 gm.

For room temperatures the Mason jars were kept in the
milling room. For the higher temperature the jars were put
in a specially made box with a thermostatic control, and

for tempering at $6^{\circ}C$, the samples were kept in the large refrigerating room of the Dairy department. The wheat was adjusted to these temperatures before the tempering water was added, and kept at that temperature during the entire tempering period. However, the milling was done at room temperature which varied between 14° and $17^{\circ}C$.

In performing experiments of this nature it is difficult to control or distinguish between the losses from evaporation and those due to the mechanical operation. The total loss during the milling and sifting operations can be obtained by adding the weights of the different stocks and subtracting the sum from the weight of the original wheat ground, which was 500 gm. Table IV shows an example of the experimental data obtained for each tempering period.

From all the data obtained as shown in Table IV the averages of the three trials were computed in each case, and Tables V and VI give the averages. The figures in Table V show the weight of the products obtained in the process of grinding these samples, the length of tempering period, the temperature of tempering, temperature and relative humidity of the room in which the samples were ground; also the gain or loss during grinding and weighing.

Table IV A sample of the experimental data obtained
for each tempering period.

Tempering time one hour. Temperature 18°C.
Weight of wheat 600 gm. Water added 20 cc.
Relative humidity 61.
Weight of wheat after tempering.
a. 620 gm.
b. 620 gm.
c. 620 gm.

Sample: No.	Weight: wheat	Over 24 W.	Over 50 G.G.	Over 70 G.G.	Through 70 G.G.	Sum:Loss
a :	500 :	221.3 :	160.0 :	56.0 :	53.8	:491.2: 8.8
b :	500 :	229.0 :	160.0 :	56.5 :	54.0	:499.5: 1.5
c :	500 :	229.95:	159.7 :	52.8 :	52.8	:494.8: 5.2
Average	:	226.6 :	159.9 :	54.8 :	53.5	:494.8: 5.2

Per cent Moisture

a :	16.73 :	17.48:	15.98:	16.15 :	16.68
b :	16.98 :	17.58:	16.30:	16.42 :	16.46
c :	16.95 :	18.24:	16.17:	16.24 :	16.37
Average 16.88 :	17.76:	16.15:	16.27 :	16.50	

The three temperatures at which the wheat was tempered were 6°C., 18°C. and 40°C. The mean room temperature during the grinding was 18° when grinding the wheat tempered at temperatures higher or lower than that of the room, and 18° for the wheat tempered at room temperature. The mean relative humidity was 62, 59, and 64 per cent respectively.

The loss which is shown in the last column of Table V. is very small in all cases. The mean loss for the 6°C. tempered wheat was 1.0 gm. or 0.2 per cent; for the 18°C. it was 3.1 gm. or 0.62 per cent, and for the 40°C tempered wheat it was 6.5 gm., or 1.3 per cent, or the loss increased with the temperature of the wheat during tempering as these samples were not cooled before grinding. This shows the greater part of the loss was due to evaporation, and that the mechanical losses were small.

The mean weights show that as the temperature for tempering was increased, more of the fine products were obtained and fewer of the coarse. We will consider the overs of the 50 G.G. as sizings, the overs of the 70 G.G. as coarse middlings, and the throughs of the 70 G.G. as fine middlings. The average amount of fine middlings produced by tempering at the low temperature of 6°C was 51.2 gm.; at 18°C 56.8 gm., and at 40°C 63.2 gm. The average amount of coarse middlings produced by tempering at 6°C. was 53 gm., at 18°C. 56.3 gm., and at 40°C. it was 60.7 gm. This shows

Table V   Distribution of grinding.

Time of tempering of hours.	Temperature of tempering °C.	Temperature of room °C.	Relative humidity.	Grams per 100 gm. of wheat.					
				Over 24 W.	Over 50 G.G.	Over 70 G.G.	Through	Sum	Loss
1	6	17	64	250.1	156.3	48.8	44.3	499.5	0.5
2	6	18	56	243.4	157.8	50.6	47.2	498.5	1.1
4	6	18	56	341.0	158.7	51.6	49.6	500.9	.9*
8	6	16	63	253.5	158.8	53.2	52.1	497.6	2.4
16	6	15	66	222.4	165.6	56.7	55.7	500.0	0.0
24	6	14	67	218.8	163.2	57.3	58.3	497.6	2.4
Mean		16	62	234.9	160.1	53.0	51.2	499.0	1.0
1	18	18	61	226.6	159.9	54.8	53.5	494.8	5.2
2	18	18	56	230.6	159.5	54.8	53.9	498.8	1.2
4	18	18	60	227.2	158.1	55.4	57.2	495.9	4.1
8	18	18	60	228.2	153.3	57.8	58.0	497.3	2.7
16	18	17	60	219.9	158.0	58.7	60.0	496.3	3.7
24	18	18	56	227.7	163.9	58.1	58.3	498.0	2.0
Mean		18	59	226.7	157.1	56.3	56.8	496.9	3.1
1	40	17	60	220.3	150.7	58.5	61.1	490.7	9.3
2	40	16	63	220.5	142.5	62.8	66.8	492.6	5.5
4	40	16	63	234.6	180.3	62.8	66.8	494.5	5.5
8	40	16	64	229.7	153.4	63.0	66.8	491.8	8.1
16	40	15	66	224.2	155.9	58.0	57.8	495.3	4.7
24	40	15	57	220.0	155.8	60.4	59.9	495.9	4.1
Mean	40	16	64	223.2	146.4	60.75	63.2	493.5	6.5

*gain.

a constant increase in coarse and fine middlings when
tempering at higher temperatures. The mean amount of sizings obtained when tempering at 5°C. was 160 gm., at 18°C.
157.1 gm., and 40°C. 144.4 gm. This shows a constant
decrease in sizings as the temperature was increased during
tempering. The mean amount of bran and endosperm left in
contact was at 5°C. 234.9 gm., at 18°C. 226.7 gm., and at
40°C. 223.2 gm. This indicates that temperature helps
mellow the endosperm and toughen the bran.

The length of time used in tempering showed a marked
effect at 5°C., since with the longer time of tempering
more sizing, coarse and fine middlings were produced. This
effect is also slightly noticeable for the wheat tempered
at 18°C., but at 40°C. no differences could be detected in
the weight of products. This means that the desired effect
of the tempering water is produced in a much shorter time
at higher temperatures.

Table VI shows the figures for the moisture content of
wheat, the overs and throughs of the sieves for the
different samples. These samples were taken as soon as
possible after grinding and placed in air tight bottles
where they were kept until the moisture tests were made.
These figures are the average from each of the three samples
milled. The data show that the moisture content of the

Table VI Penetration of water in wheat under various conditions of time and temperature.

Time of temper	Temperature of tempering °C	Temperature of room °C	Relative humidity	Whole wheat	Moisture per cent.			
					Over 94%.	Over 500 d.	Over 500 d. to 0.0.	Through 70 0.0.
1 hour	6	17	64	16.41	17.09	16.90	14.97	14.47
8 hours	6	18	56	16.41	17.44	16.63	14.14	14.43
4 hours	6	18	56	16.44	17.41	16.31	14.27	14.49
8 hours	6	18	63	16.44	17.71	16.57	14.44	14.49
16 hours	6	14	64	16.70	17.47	16.36	14.19	14.38
24 hours	6	15	67	16.79	17.47	16.04	14.38	14.40
Mean		16	68					
1 hour	18	18	61	16.88	17.78	16.16	14.97	16.50
8 hours	18	18	56	16.91	17.45	16.13	14.11	14.07
4 hours	18	18	60	16.58	17.46	16.47	14.98	16.40
8 hours	18	18	90	17.08	17.50	14.39	16.51	16.43
16 hours	18	17	56	17.61	17.68	16.68	16.49	16.68
24 hours	18	18	99	16.74	17.17	16.39	16.69	16.61
Mean		18	89	16.85	17.49	16.55	16.54	16.43
1 hour	40	17	90	16.88	17.47	16.61	16.19	16.09
8 hours	40	16	83	16.88	17.10	14.21	16.20	16.58
4 hours	40	16	83	16.87	16.78	15.85	15.92	16.06
8 hours	40	17	84	16.51	16.47	16.65	15.61	15.66
16 hours	40	14	86	16.73	17.08	14.41	15.57	16.61
24 hours	40	15	97	16.85	16.94	16.35	16.10	16.84
Mean		16	84	16.67	16.99	16.06	16.10	16.19

wheat samples was rather uniform. They also show that in all cases the bran contained a larger per cent of moisture than the endosperm. In fact, in every case the moisture content of the bran was greater than that of the wheat. At the lowest temperature of 5°C., the moisture content of the sizings was less than that of the finer middlings. This indicates that the moisture was not evenly distributed through the interior of the grain. After two hours at 18°C. the moisture seemed to be evenly distributed throughout the endosperm, as shown by the moisture content of the sizings and coarse and fine middlings. At 40°C. a fairly uniform distribution was found at one hour, as indicated by moisture content of sizings, coarse and fine middlings.

The following conclusions may be drawn from the experiments with the rate of water penetration of wheat:

1. The wheat kernel is not enclosed in a non permeable membrane, but absorbs water freely through the entire bran surface.

2. The bran coat has a greater affinity for water than the endosperm of the wheat.

3. Temperature influences the rate at which water may enter the wheat.

4. At 18°C. or above, the water had penetrated the wheat kernel in 2 hours, and was evenly distributed throughout the endosperm.

EXPERIMENTS ON SMALL EXPERIMENTAL MILL

The effects of temperature on wheat tempering were studied first on the small experimental mill for the economic reason that it could be attacked from many more angles at less expense. The disposal of the products manufactured did not enter into the question as they were easily blended in with other products on the large mill. The problem, influence of temperature on wheat tempering was attacked from five angles on the small mill.

The effect of temperature and length of tempering period on the distribution of grinding, as measured by the per cent of extraction done by each break roll in the process of separating the endosperm from the bran.

2. The effect of temperature and the length of tempering period on the amount of sizings and middlings produced.

3. The effect of temperature and the length of tempering period on the amount of break flour produced by the different breaks.

4. The effect of temperature and the length of tempering period on the ash content of the different break flours.

5. The effect of temperature and the length of tempering period on the amount of power required to separate the bran from the endosperm during the breaking process.

A lot of well-blended, hard red winter wheat of a known
moisture content was used for these experiments. The wheat
was cleaned and scoured before weighing out portions for
each test. For each test 1000 gm. of wheat was placed in
tin cans with tight lids. Enough water was added to bring
the moisture content up to 15.5 per cent as determined by
the Brown Duvel method. The periods of tempering were $\frac{1}{4}, \frac{1}{2}$,
1, 2, 4, 6, and 16 hours, and the time of tempering was so
regulated that the wheat could be milled at the expiration
of the tempering period set for each test. A relative
humidity of approximately 50 per cent varying only one or
two per cent, was kept during the entire experiment, and a
temperature of approximately 27°C. was maintained.

For the room temperature, 27°C., the cans were kept
in the milling room. For the higher temperature the cans
were kept in a specially made box with a thermostatic control. The wheat was adjusted to these temperatures before
the tempering water was added, and the temperature maintained
constant during the entire tempering process. However, the
milling was done at room temperature which varied between
25°C. and 28°C.

The samples were ground on an experimental mill
equipped with a pair of 6 by 6 inch rolls, corrugated with
a modified Dawson cut. A differential of $2\frac{1}{2}$ to 1 was used
for grinding, and a constant feed was maintained on these

rolls for each individual break. The mill was driven by a
three horse power motor which gave ample power at all times
during the tests. Since accuracy in setting the rolls was
important an instrument was made which magnified the movement of the rolls sixteen times. The distance used between
the rolls for the different break settings was first .028
inch, second .012 inch, third .006 inch, and fourth .002
inch. These were kept constant in all the different tests
made.

The ground sample was sifted on an experimental sifter
which is equipped with an automatic time regulator. The
action of this sifter is similar to the action of the sifter
on the large mill, and the results were comparative since
all samples were sifted the same length of time, two
minutes. The cloth used in each case was similar to those
used on the large four break automatic mill as shown in
Table VII.

Table VII Cloth used in experimental sifter.

Break 1		Break 2		Break 3		Break 4
20 Wire	:	20 Wire	:	24 Wire	:	18 Wire
32 "	:	32 "	:	36 "	:	26 "
50 G.G.	:	50 G.G.	:	54 G.G.	:	44 "
70 G.G.	:	70 G.G.	:	72 G.G.	:	70 G.G.
13 XX	:	12 XX	:	12 XX	:	13 XX

The overs of each sieve were weighed on a Torsion balance sensitive to .01 gms, and the per cent calculated on the basis of the original sample of 1000 gm. In other words by moving the decimal point one place to the left in the weight column it will give the per cent of the original sample.

The milling of the wheat for each temperature and period of tempering was done in duplicate, and repeated when a variation indicated error in one sample or the other. The weights for the overs and break flour for the duplicate trials were averaged and the averages taken as the overs and break flour for that particular test. The ash determinations of the break flour were made on composite samples of the duplicate tests for each individual break. Table VIII is a sample of the data collected from which the following tables were made.

Results of Experiment

The effect of temperature and the length of tempering period on the distribution of grinding as measured by the per cent extraction done by each break roll in the process of separating the endosperm from the bran is shown in Table IX, while Table X shows the total extraction produced on each break.

Table VIII   Data collected on wheat tempered at 40°C.

Moisture in wheat 15 per cent.   Relative humidity 51 per
Moisture at rolls 15.3 per cent. cent.

	Sieve No.	Weight of first sample	Weight of second sample	Average weight	Power kilowatts
1st. Break	30 W.:	772	777	776.5	1st. trial 180
	32 W.:	87	84	85.5	2nd. trial 160
	500 G.:	62	60	61.5	Average 170
	70 G.G.:	37	35	36.0	
	13XX :	32	32	32.0	
	Flour:	6	6	6.0	
2nd. Break					
	30 W.:	365	360	362.5	1st. trial 80
	32 W.:	86	74	80.0	2nd. trial 80
	50 G.G.:	172	185	178.5	Average 80
	700 G.:	66	85	75.5	
	13XX :	56	65	60.0	
	Flour:	19	24	21.5	
3rd. Break					
	24 W.:	245	232	237.5	1st. trial 60
	36 W.:	16	16	16.0	2nd. trial 50
	54 G.G.:	28	22	25.0	Average 55
	72 G.G.:	30	26.5	28.3	
	12XX :	35	32	32.5	
	Flour:	8	10	9.0	
4th. Break					
	18 W.:	165	165	165.0	1st. trial 40
	26 W.:	36	39	37.5	2nd. trial 30
	44 W.:	14	15	14.5	Average 35
	70 G.G.:	11	9	10.0	
	13XX :	15	14	14.5	
	Flour:	2	2	2.0	

Table IX   Per cent extraction on the different breaks.

Temperature °C.	Length of temper hours.						
	½	¾	1	2	4	6	16
First Break							
27	20.5	20.3	20.8	21.3	20.0	22.0	22.3
40	22.5	20.5	24.0	21.0	20.6	20.7	21.5
50	23.7	23.5	24.5	23.5	23.8	20.0	22.3
60	13.3	21.3	17.5	15.6	16.3	16.0	15.8
Average	20.0	21.4	21.7	20.3	20.2	19.7	20.5
Largest Deviation	6.7	2.1	4.2	4.7	3.9	3.7	4.7
Second Break							
27	38.0	39.7	39.7	40.0	39.0	38.0	36.5
40	42.2	41.3	35.0	33.7	36.6	36.2	38.7
50	38.0	37.5	39.0	36.5	35.5	38.8	39.2
60	44.2	34.2	36.8	34.7	37.5	36.0	40.0
Average	40.6	38.2	37.6	36.2	37.2	37.2	38.6
Largest Deviation	3.6	4.0	2.6	3.8	1.8	1.2	2.1
Third Break							
27	16.0	16.0	15.3	14.2	17.5	14.3	16.0
40	11.5	10.7	14.0	16.5	14.8	16.5	15.2
50	13.8	13.8	11.5	15.0	14.1	14.2	12.8
60	16.3	14.8	15.8	20.8	16.7	19.5	17.2
Average	14.4	13.8	14.4	16.6	15.7	16.1	15.6
Largest Deviation	2.9	3.1	2.9	4.2	1.8	3.4	2.8
Fourth Break							
27	9.5	9.5	9.6	9.3	9.0	12.0	11.5
40	8.2	9.5	9.8	10.1	10.4	10.0	9.7
50	11.4	11.6	10.0	10.5	10.8	10.6	11.8
60	10.2	12.3	11.0	13.0	11.8	12.8	10.8
Average	9.8	10.7	10.1	10.7	10.5	11.4	11.0
Largest Deviation	1.6	1.6	.9	2.3	1.5	1.4	1.3

Table I   Total extraction at various temperatures.

Temperature °C.	Length of temper hours						
	¼	½	1	2	4	6	16
27	84.0	85.5	85.4	85.3	85.5	86.3	86.3
40	84.4	82.0	82.8	81.5	82.2	83.4	85.1
50	86.9	86.4	85.0	85.5	84.2	83.6	86.1
60	84.0	82.3	81.1	84.1	82.3	84.3	83.8
Average	84.8	84.1	83.6	84.1	83.6	84.4	85.3
Largest Deviation	2.1	2.3	2.5	2.8	1.9	1.9	1.5

In comparing the effect of temperature on the first break extraction, Table IX shows that as the temperature was increased the per cent extraction decreased for all different lengths of temper longer than ½ hour. The second and third breaks do not show any direct trend, the fluctuation is within the error due to mechanical operation. For the higher temperature fourth break shows that the bran and endosperm did not separate in the former breaks as readily as at the lower temperatures.

The total extraction of middlings as produced by all four breaks, Table X, shows no decided trend in the amount of middlings produced as the temperature was increased or as the length of the tempering period was extended. The largest deviation from the average at any tempering period was 2.8 per cent at 40°C. tempered 2 hours.

The effect of temperature and the length of tempering period on the amount of different size middlings produced is shown in Table XI. The overs of the 32 and 36 wire was considered as sizings; the overs of the 50 and 54 grit gauze as coarse middlings; the overs of the 70 and 72 grit gauze as medium middlings; and the overs of the 12 and 13 XX silk as fine middlings. The amount of sizings and medium middlings did not vary in any direct trend but only had a slight fluctuation at 27°C. The amount of coarse middlings decreased slightly with the increased tempering period,

Table XI Influence of time and temperature on size of
middlings.

Temperature C.		Length of temper hours.						
		1/4	1/2	1	2	4	6	12

Sizings

27	:	208	: 200	: 192	: 181	: 180	: 187	:203
40	:	182	: 170	: 195	: 160	: 150	: 151	:146
50	:	210	: 184	: 170	: 163	: 160	: 132	:146
60	:	185	: 174	: 141	: 135	: 126	: 120	:118

Coarse Middlings

27	:	270	: 268	: 257	: 264	: 259	: 256	:252
40	:	265	: 254	223	: 230	: 223	: 222	:223
50	:	267	239	: 243	: 238	229	: 229	:231
60	:	248	220	· 213	: 191	201	: 192	:191

Medium Middlings

27	:	145	: 145	: 149	: 154	: 144	: 140	:138
40	:	150	: 147	: 140	: 150	: 157	: 157	:173
50	:	139	: 147	: 152	: 153	: 152	: 156	:160
60	:	148	: 144	: 157	: 145	: 156	: 165	:162

Fine Middlings

27	:	114	: 116	: 125	: 126	: 125	: 125	:124
40	:	135	142	: 149	: 155	: 163	: 165	:173
50	:	126	142	: 146	: 152	: 152	: 150	:160
60	:	135	149	: 167	: 185	: 172	: 192	:195

while the amount of fine middlings had a slight increase
with the longer tempering periods. At the higher temperatures the amount of sizings and coarse middlings decreased
with the temperature and longer tempering periods, while
the amount of fine middlings increased with the temperature
and length of tempering period. As the temperature is
increased the endosperm becomes mellow in a shorter time and
similar results are produced in a longer period of tempering at a lower temperature.

The effect of temperature and the length of tempering
period on amount of break flour produced by the different
breaks is shown in Table XII. The higher temperatures
seemed to cut down the amount of break flour produced on
first break. The long tempering periods produced more break
flour on second and third breaks due to the mellowness of
the endosperm. The amount of flour produced on fourth
break followed no direct trend.

The quality of the break flours was measured by
determining the ash content which is given in Table XIII.
The ash content of the first break flour fluctuated so
great that no comparison can be made. However, the ash
content of second break flour was lower at the higher
temperatures and after $\frac{1}{2}$ hour showed no direct trend. The
extreme short temper of $\frac{1}{2}$ hour had a higher ash content than

Table XII Amount of break flour produced.

Temperature °C.	Length of temper hours						
	½	¾	1	2	4	6	16
First Break							
27	6.0	5.0	7.5	7.0	5.0	7.5	9.5
40	3.0	4.5	7.0	4.5	3.8	5.0	6.5
50	4.8	8.0	7.5	7.8	8.0	6.0	8.5
60	2.0	3.5	2.5	8.0	1.8	1.0	1.5
Average	4.9	6.3	6.1	5.3	5.8	4.9	6.0
Largest Deviation	2.9	2.8	3.6	3.3	4.0	3.9	4.5
Second Break							
27	18.5	18.0	19.5	28.0	19.0	20.0	16.5
40	21.5	20.0	19.0	17.0	22.0	21.0	28.4
50	17.0	22.5	24.5	23.8	22.5	25.5	31.8
60	20.5	16.0	20.0	20.0	25.0	24.5	36.3
Average	19.4	19.1	20.8	20.7	22.1	22.8	28.3
Largest Deviation	2.1	3.6	1.8	3.1	3.1	2.8	11.8
Third Break							
	13.5	13.0	13.5	14.5	12.0	12.0	15.0
	9.0	8.5	13.5	13.8	13.0	17.5	18.0
27	13.0	15.5	12.0	18.0	16.0	18.0	16.3
60	14.5	12.5	15.0	25.0	18.5	23.5	23.5
Average	12.5	12.4	13.5	17.8	14.9	17.8	18.2
Largest Deviation	3.5	3.9	1.5	7.2	3.6	5.8	5.3
Fourth Break							
27	5.5	5.0	3.0	4.5	7.5	10.0	8.0
40	2.0	3.5	5.5	4.8	3.8	3.8	3.5
50	5.0	5.3	2.5	3.5	4.8	5.5	6.5
60	3.5	5.0	4.0	5.0	4.5	5.5	3.5
Average	4.0	4.7	3.8	4.5	5.1	6.2	5.4
Largest Devaition	2.0	1.2	1.7	1.0	2.4	3.8	2.6

the longer tempers. Third break had the lowest ash at
four hours temper in all cases except at 60°C. in which the
one hour temper was the lowest for that temperature. The
ash content of the fourth break flour showed no direct
trends but a general fluctuation.

The effect of temperature and the length of tempering
period on the amount of power in kilowatts required to
separate the bran from the endosperm during the breaking
process, is shown in Table XIV. The first break which
breaks the grain open, required more than twice the amount
of power than was used in any of the other breaks. At the
higher temperatures it took nearly three times as much
power as used on second break. The 1 hour temper at 27°C.
required 190 kilowatts, and for the 16 hour temper 295
kilowatts; at 60°C. the 1 hour temper used 200 kilowatts,
and the 16 hour temper required 355 kilowatts. On the
three remaining breaks the power requirements did not show
any trends. The second break required approximately 80
kilowatts; third break 60 kilowatts; fourth break 50
kilowatts.

The lower temperatures did not show any material
difference in the power requirement, but the higher temperatures at longer periods of tempes showed marked increased
amount of power required to open the grain.

Continued.

Table XIII Ash in break flour.

Temperature °C	Length of temper hours						
	¼	½	1	2	4	6	16
First Break							
27	.77	.76	.70	.69	.71	.78	.74
40	.70	.67	.71	.67	.64	.66	.76
50	.66	.63	.81	.65	.72	.68	.72
60	.68	.80		.73	.71	.76	.67
Second Break							
27	.66	.64	.57	.57	.60	.61	.60
40	.60	.59	.58	.60	.54	.59	.58
50	.62	.55	.57	.56	.54	.55	.56
60	.61	.55	.55	.56	.56	.57	.56
Third Break							
27	.60	.63	.56	.59	.54	.60	.54
40	.68	.63	.62	.62	.56	.61	.66
50	.66	.62	.60	.60	.58	.63	.65
60	.64	.62	.59	.60	.66	.63	.70
Fourth Break							
27	.72	.83	.80	.79	.64	.69	.64
40	.92	.72	.76	.76	.76	.79	.88
50	.76	.87	.82	.90	.82	.79	.86
60	.83	.80	.90	.84	.80	.83	.90

Table XIV Power used in grinding, kilowatt hours.

Temperature °C.	Length of temper hours						
	½	¾	1	2	4	6	16
First Break							
27	175	170	190	200	210	300	220
40	170	180	220	210	235	230	250
50	190	245	210	290	275	265	295
60	165	255	200	190	340	300	335
Second Break							
27	90	75	85	80	93	96	100
40	90	70	60	75	70	65	80
50	75	80	85	70	80	75	85
60	70	70	95	65	80	80	90
Third Break							
27	55	50	60	55	60	60	66
40	55	35	60	55	50	65	90
50	65	70	40	60	57	55	65
60	60	55	55	55	60	65	70
Fourth Break							
27	55	60	65	60	60	70	56
40	35	40	30	40	50	55	45
50	75	80	50	65	75	55	75
60	50	50	50	45	60	55	60

LARGE MILL EXPERIMENTS

A few tests were conducted on the large experimental mill in order to check the results obtained on the small mill for the effect of temperature during tempering in the conditioning of wheat for milling. Ten to 15 bushel samples of dark hard winter wheat were used in these tests.

In two of these tests a high quality wheat of the 1929 crop was used. This wheat graded number two dark hard winter having a moisture content of 12 per cent. Two tests were made from a blend of half 1929 wheat, and the other half a weak 1928 wheat which contained heat damaged and weevil eaten kernels. This latter wheat had 13 per cent moisture. Two tests were made on number two dark hard winter wheat bought from export grain in Galveston, Texas. The one sample was heated to 60°C. for sterilization, then both were shipped to Kansas State Agricultural College for milling.

When conducting these tests a 5 bushel sample was milled before starting the test in order to get the mill in proper working condition. The sample under observation was then milled. The length of tempering period was 3 hours in all cases eliminating this variable.

Tempering was done at three different temperatures in addition to room temperature. Sound wheat was heated to

44°C. for three hours during tempering; a blend of sound
wheat and damaged wheat was sealed to 12°C. and tempered
for three hours at that temperature; expert wheat sterilized
by heating to 60°C. for five minutes was tempered at 24°C.
For each of the three cases similar wheat was tempered at
24°C. or room temperature and milled for comparison.

The same system of cleaning was used in all tests;
receiving separator, milling separator, Carter disc,
horizontal scourer, heater (when used), and a dampener.
The wheat was then placed in specially constructed tank
in which the temperature could be maintained as that at the
time of tempering. At the end of the tempering period it
was scoured and then run through a cooler, cooling to 24°C.
just before going to the break rolls. The humidity control
was started two hours before starting the mill in order to
have the temperature and humidity constant before grinding
the preliminary sample.

The breaks and reduction rolls were set during the
grinding of the preliminary sample and not changed during
the experiment with the exception of a few of the reduction
rolls which heated and formed rings on the rolls.

The effect of temperature on wheat during tempering was
studied by the following measurements: Samples were caught
under the break rolls and sifted on a Rotomatic sifter to
determine the per cent extraction and size of middlings

produced as determined by the weights of the overs of the
various sieves used in sifting. The power used for grinding
was determined by the use of a wattmeter connected to the
motor which drove the rolls. The various flour streams were
caught for 10 minutes, weighed, and bottle samples taken
for moisture and ash determinations. Samples of the
patent and clear flour were taken for moisture and ash
determinations, and baking tests were made on the patent
flour for comparisons.

Results of Large Mill Experiments

The samples caught for sifting to determine the per
cent extraction and size of middlings were taken from both
ends of the break roll under observation, and without
allowing the sampling pan to run over as the coarse stock
would roll off the pan and the fine material sift down
among that already in pan. The weighing of all samples
and overs of the various sieves was done on a torsion
balance sensitive to one tenth of a gram. The sifting
of samples on the Rotomatic sifter was done on a stack of
sieves similar to that used on the large mill for each
break. Two minutes time was allowed for sifting as was
done in connection with the work done on the experimental
mill. After each sifting the overs of each sieve and the

break flour were weighed and from these weights the per
cent overs of each sieve and the break flour were determined.

In Table XV are the data obtained when sifting samples
caught from the wheat that had been tempered at 44°C. In
In column one is shown the cloth used in sifting for each
break. Column two gives the weight of the sample caught
and the weight of the overs of each sieve as well as the
throughs of flour cloth. Column three gives the weight of
wheat necessary to produce the weight of sample caught for
that individual break. Column four shows the per cent
overs of the various sieves and the per cent break flour.
Column five gives the per cent extraction produced on the
individual breaks.

In the case of the second and subsequent breaks, the
weight of the wheat required to produce the sample taken,
as given in column three, is computed by dividing the weight
of the sample caught by the per cent overs on the top sieve
for the previous break. This gives the correct value since
in each case the per cent overs is figured on the basis of
the original wheat, and the overs of the top wire for one
break constitute the sample which passes to the next
break.

Table XVI gives the per cent extraction made by the
various breaks as determined by the sifting and calculated
as shown in Table XV.

Table IV Data and calculations for wheat tempered
at 44°C.

	Weight in grams	Weight of wheat	Per cent overs	Per cent Extraction
1st. Break				
Wt. of sample:	323 :	323 :	100 :	22.8
20 wire	252 :	:	78.2:	
32 wire	24 :	:	7.4:	
50 G.G.	23 :	:	7.1:	
70 G.G.	10 :	:	3.1:	
13 XX	10 :	:	3.1:	
Flour	2 :	:	.6:	
2nd. Break				
Wt. of sample:	331 :	424 :	78.2:	43.5
20 wire	147 :	:	34.7:	
32 wire	29 :	:	6.8:	
50 G.G.	80 :	:	18.8:	
70 G.G.	35 :	:	8.3:	
12 XX	30 :	:	7.1:	
Flour	8 :	:	1.9:	
3rd. Break				
Wt. of sample:	216 :	680 :	34.7:	14.9
24 wire	134 :	:	19.8:	
36 wire	16 :	:	2.4:	
60 G.G.	25 :	:	3.7:	
72 G.G.	15 :	:	2.2:	
12 XX	17 :	:	2.5:	
Flour	4 :	:	.6:	
4th. Break				
Wt. of sample:	200 :	1001 :	19.8:	4.9
18 wire	104 :	:	10.2:	
26 wire	32 :	:	3.1:	
44 wire	16 :	:	1.6:	
70 G.G.	31 :	:	3.0:	
13 XX	14 :	:	1.4:	
Flour	2 :	:	.2:	

Table XVI Per cent extraction on the various breaks.

Kind of wheat	Tempering temperature in °C.	First break	Second break	Third break	Fourth break	Bran and shorts
Mixed :	12	:26.4 :	41.0	: 11.6 :	5.2 :	14.8
Mixed :	24	:26.0 :	35.0	: 13.7 :	5.5 :	19.8
1929 :	44	:21.8 :	43.5	: 14.9 :	4.9 :	14.9
Car :	36	:22.0 :	39.4	: 16.8 :	3.2 :	18.6
Export :	24*	:23.4 :	41.5	: 12.7 :	5.4 :	14.0
Export :	24	:25.7 :	41.7	: 11.7 :	6.5 :	14.4

* Sterilized at 60°C.

In Table XVI the first column shows the type of wheat; the second column the temperature of wheat; columns three, four, five, and six the per cent extraction on the four breaks and column seven the bran plus the shorts over the 44 wire on fourth break. The per cent extraction shows no general trend as to the amount of endosperm separated from the bran. The excess amount of bran and shorts in the two cases is thought to be an accidental variation.

The size of the middlings produced as determined by sifting sample is shown in Table XVII. Table XVII shows the per cent of different size middlings and sizings produced by the different samples. The per cent sizings and middlings were determined from the data tables similar to Table XV by adding the percentages of similar size products

Table XVII Per cent of different size middlings.

Kind of wheat	Tempering temperature in °C.	Sizings	Coarse middlings	Medium middlings	Fine middlings	Flour
Mixed	12	30.8	28.6	17.6	15.3	4.4
Mixed	24	18.9	24.8	19.2	15.7	3.4
1939	44	16.6	29.6	16.6	13.6	3.5
Car	24	16.2	29.6	16.0	13.1	4.6
Export	24*	23.8	32.2	13.2	11.3	4.1
Export	24	21.1	31.1	13.9	12.4	4.3

*Sterilized at 60°C.

from the different breaks. The overs of the 32 and 36 wire
on first, second and third breaks were calculated as
sizings; the overs of the 50 and 60 grit gauze on first,
second and third breaks as coarse middlings; the overs of
the 70 and 72 grit gauze on all four breaks as medium
middlings; the overs of the 12 and 13 XX on all four breaks
as fine middlings; and the throughs of the 12 and 13 XX as
flour. By this method the mellowness of the endosperm
should be shown. The trials are so few in number that no
direct comparison can be shown, but the sold wheat seemed
to produce more coarse middlings than the wheat tempered
at a higher temperature. In the case where the export
wheat was sterilized it shows practically no difference

when compared to the wheat that had not been heated or
sterilized.

The effect of the temperature on the power requirement
is shown by the number of kilowatts used to grind one
bushel of wheat which is shown in Table XVIII.

Table XVIII Power required to grind one bushel
of wheat.

Kind of wheat	Tempering temperature	Kilowatts per bushel of wheat
Mixed	12	1.32
Mixed	24	1.23
1929	44	1.29
Car	24	1.21
Export	24*	1.22
Export	24	1.20

* Sterilized at 60°C.

This shows that in case of the mixed wheat less power
was used for the wheat tempered at room temperature than
at cooler temperatures. The 1929 wheat required more power
when tempered at 44°C. than at room temperature. This was
also true in case of the export wheat. In explaining these
two trends the cool wheat had not mellowed the endosperm,
which required more power to reduce it into flour. The
higher than room temperature required more power because
the grain was tougher and the endosperm was slightly sticky
which made it difficult to mill.

Table XIX gives the weight of the flour caught from the various flour streams. These samples were caught for 10 minute periods and the weights recorded. The amount of flour produced in 10 minutes seemed to vary considerably on the different parts of the mill, probably due to the fact that these samples were not milled on the same days. The two export samples which were milled one after the other have almost identical amounts of total flour for the 10 minute periods, but the various streams have fluctuated considerably in the different tests, which makes it impossible to form any definite conclusions from these measures. The error due to the short period of time while the samples were caught was greater than the difference due to a variation in the effect of temperature upon the amount of flour produced.

In Tables XX and XXI are presented the ash and moisture determinations of the various flour streams produced while milling these different samples. There appears to be very little difference between the samples tempered at room temperature or higher, but the sample tempered at $12^{\circ}C$. has less moisture in the finished products and higher ash. Both of these are undesirable. Hence, it appears that wheat tempered at $12^{\circ}C$. or below will produce a flour of higher ash and lower moisture content than a flour tempered at $24^{\circ}C$. or above.

Table XIX Weights of flour streams for ten minutes.

Flour Streams	Mixed wheat		1939 wheat		Export wheat	
	12°C.	24°C.	44°C.	24°C.	60°C.	24°C.
1st. Break	725	570	312	470	475	412
2nd. Break	950	700	682	585	615	719
3rd. Break	780	685	462	575	545	397
4th. Break	725	360	157	485	655	472
Sizings	1400	1175	1332	1105	2020	1635
1st. Middlings	3890	3960	2702	5105	3770	4787
2nd. Middlings	4015	2800	4045	2380	5065	3210
3rd. Middlings	4945	5650	4430	4515	5295	6290
4th. Middlings	6390	8070	5782	3945	4165	4540
5th. Middlings	3365	1450	1887	1965	2320	2900
1st Tailings	1405	1095	980	1375	1185	1030
2nd Tailings	3685	2800	1710	1730	2150	2450
Reel	2805	2700	1502	2100	2035	2389
Total	35240	28435	22953	23935	31295	31231

Table XX Ash in the different flour streams.

Flour Streams	Mixed wheat		Hard wheat		Export wheat	
	15°C.	26°C.	44°C.	26°C.	60°C.	24°C.
1st. Break	.75	.85	.48	.43	.67	.72
2nd. Break	.64	.62	.60	.45	.61	.68
3rd. Break	.75	.58	.59	.46	.68	.74
4th. Break	.89	.85	.88	.64	.84	.87
Sizings	.46	.42	.34	.36	.35	.35
1st. Middlings	.43	.41	.35	.37	.35	.36
2nd. Middlings	.44	.43	.36	.37	.34	.34
3rd. Middlings	.41	.40	.38	.34	.31	.31
4th Middlings	.43	.44	.36	.36	.36	.36
5th. Middlings	.47	.44	.37	.41	.36	.41
1st. Tailings	.54	.50	.41	.42	.45	.48
2nd. Tailings	.53	.51	.45	.47	.45	.51
Reel	.70	.65	.62	.60	.66	.80
Patent	.52	.45	.35	.37	.37	.36
Clear	.84	.65	.56	.54	.63	.73

Table XXI Moisture in different flour streams.

Flour Streams	Mixed wheat		Hard wheat		Export wheat	
	15°C.	25°C.	50°C.	95°C.	50°C.	95°C.
1st. Break	14.6	14.5	14.6	15.0	13.2	13.5
2nd. Break	14.6	15.0	14.5	15.6	13.0	13.6
3rd. Break	14.7	15.5	14.6	15.3	13.0	13.5
4th. Break	14.5	14.1	14.4	14.9	12.9	13.2
Sizings	14.0	14.3	14.3	14.6	12.7	13.5
1st. Middlings	13.8	14.4	14.5	15.0	12.7	13.5
2nd. Middlings	13.6	13.8	14.0	14.6	12.5	13.3
3rd. Middlings	13.1	13.4	13.7	14.2	12.3	12.9
4th. Middlings	13.0	12.1	13.5	13.5	11.8	12.6
5th. Middlings	11.7	12.9	13.5	14.6	12.0	12.5
1st. Tailings	13.5	13.3	13.5	13.7	12.8	13.9
2nd. Tailings	11.7	12.5	13.1	13.0	11.6	12.2
Reel	11.6	12.4	13.1	13.2	12.0	12.4
Patent	11.8	13.1	13.8	13.5	12.8	13.0
Clear	11.1	12.3	13.6	13.1	12.1	12.1

Baking tests were made on the patent flour samples for the various periods using a standard baking formula which is used in making the baking test in this laboratory. The results of the tests are given in Table XXII.

Table XXII Baking results of the patent flours.

Kind of flour	Tempering temperature.	Loaf Volume	Color	Texture
Mixed wheat :	12	: 1560	: 96 dark :	97
Mixed wheat :	24	: 1490	: 96 :	98
1929 Car :	24	: 1560	: 98	98
" " :	44	: 1560	: 98	97
Export wheat:	24	: 1600	: 97 :	98
" " :	24*	: 1560	: 98	97

*Sterilised at 60°C.

The smaller loaf volume obtained from the flour from the mixed wheat was expected since the gluten of this flour was weaker, while in the other flours the variation was small.

CONCLUSIONS

It may be concluded from these experiments that:

1. Increased temperature accelerates the rate of water penetration in wheat.

2. No portion of the wheat kernel has the character-istics of a non-permeable membrane.

3. Milling wheat at low temperatures produces flour
of higher ash content, due to pulverizing the bran.

4. High temperatures maintained for a long tempering
period are detrimental because of the unfavorable changes
in the physical characteristics of the grain.

5. The best temperature and period for tempering is
related to the characteristics of the wheat. This is a
subject for further investigation.

LITERATURE CITED

Amos, P.A.
    1920 Process of Flour Manufacture.
          Longmans' Technical Handicraft Series, 121-122.

Dunham, Robert W.
    1925 The Conditioning of Wheat Milling.
          Milling, Vol. 64, 5:677.

Kent-Jones, Dr. D.W.
    1927 Improving Flour by Physical Methods.
          The Millers Review, Vol. 91, 8:34.

Lewellen, S.J.
    1927 Effect of Milling Temperature on Flour.
          Milling, Vol. 69, 7:17-18.

McCormick, R.E.
    1930 Effect of Length of the Tempering Period on the
          Process of Milling.
          Master Thesis, Kansas State Agricultural College,
          83-84.

Simon, E.D.
    1923 Principles of Wheat Conditioning.
          Milling, Vol. 60, 6:738.

Swanson, Dr. C.O.
    1928 Effect of Heating Immature Wheat.
          The Millers Review, Vol. 92, 5:47.

Tague, E.L.
    1920 Changes Taking Place in the Tempering of Wheat.
          Journal of Agricultural Research, Vol. XX,
          271-275.

CPSIA information can be obtained
at www.ICGtesting.com
Printed in the USA
BVHW041057271218
536518BV00006B/211/P

9 780265 856284